How Your
BODY
Works

Your
Muscles
and Bones

How Your **BODY** Works

Your Muscles and Bones

Anita Ganeri

Gareth Stevens Publishing
A WORLD ALMANAC EDUCATION GROUP COMPANY

ACKNOWLEDGMENTS

With thanks to: Nicole Arellano, Nicola and Justin Mooi, Mylton Burden, Indiana Frankham, Ariadne Snowden, Courtney Thomas, and Ellen and Jack Millard.
Models from Truly Scrumptious Ltd.

Please visit our web site at: www.garethstevens.com
For a free color catalog describing Gareth Stevens Publishing's
list of high-quality books and multimedia programs, call
1-800-542-2595 (USA) or 1-800-387-3178 (Canada).
Gareth Stevens Publishing's fax: (414) 332-3567.

Library of Congress Cataloging-in-Publication Data

Ganeri, Anita, 1961-
    Your muscles and bones / by Anita Ganeri.
       p. cm. — (How your body works)
    Summary: Introduces the parts of the body that keep humans upright and on the move.
    Includes bibliographical references and index.
    ISBN 0-8368-3635-9 (lib. bdg.)
    1. Musculoskeletal system—Juvenile literature. [1. Muscular system. 2. Muscles.
3. Skeleton. 4. Bones.] I. Title. II. Series.
QP301.G3614   2003
612.7—dc21   2002036531

This North American edition first published in 2003 by
Gareth Stevens Publishing
A World Almanac Education Group Company
330 West Olive Street, Suite 100
Milwaukee, WI 53212 USA

Original edition © 2003 by Evans Brothers Limited. First published in 2003 by Evans Brothers Limited, 2A Portman Mansions, Chiltern Street, London W1U 6NR, United Kingdom. This U.S. edition published under license from Evans Brothers Limited. This U.S. edition © 2003 by Gareth Stevens, Inc. Additional end matter © 2003 by Gareth Stevens, Inc.

Designer: Mark Holt
Artwork: Julian Baker
Photography: Steve Shott
Consultant: Dr. M. Turner

Gareth Stevens Editor: Carol Ryback
Gareth Stevens Designer: Katherine A. Goedheer

Photo credits:
Science Photo Library: Professor P. Motta/Department of Anatomy/University "La Sapienza," Rome, page 10; Department of Clinical Radiology, Salisbury District Hospital, page 11; Astrid and Hanns-Frieder Michler, page 13; Philippe Plailly/Eurelios, page 20. Photograph on page 9 by Peter Millard.

Printed in the United States of America

1 2 3 4 5 6 7 8 9 07 06 05 04 03

Contents

What Makes You Move?

Think of all the ways your body moves. You can make small movements, such as blinking your eyes or sticking out your tongue. You can also hop on one leg, jump, and run. When you run, your whole body moves, all the way from your eyebrows right down to your toes. Your body is always moving, even when you are asleep. Your heart beats and your lungs breathe air in and out all of the time.

Amazing!

Your body has about 640 **muscles**. About one third of your body weight is muscle.

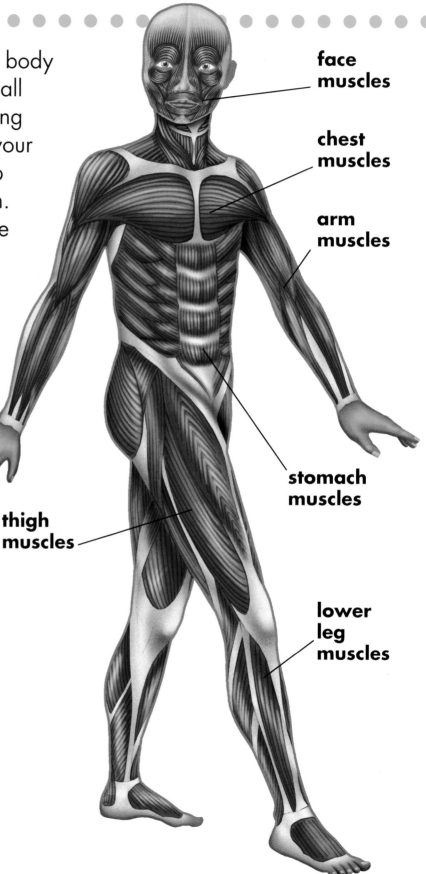

face muscles

chest muscles

arm muscles

stomach muscles

thigh muscles

lower leg muscles

You are able to move because your muscles, **bones**, brain, and **nerves** all work together. Some muscles, such as those in your arms and legs, pull on your bones to make you move. Other muscles, such as those in your face, pull on your skin to make you smile or frown.

Muscles move your eyes as you read. You also use muscles in your arm and hand to turn the pages of this book.

Your Skeleton

You have more than 200 bones inside your body. They make up your **skeleton**. When you were born, you had about 350 bones. As you grew, some of the smaller bones joined together. Your bones have different sizes and shapes — long, short, round, and flat. Each bone has a special name.

Amazing!

Your biggest, longest, and strongest bone is the bone in the top of your leg. It is called your **thigh** bone.

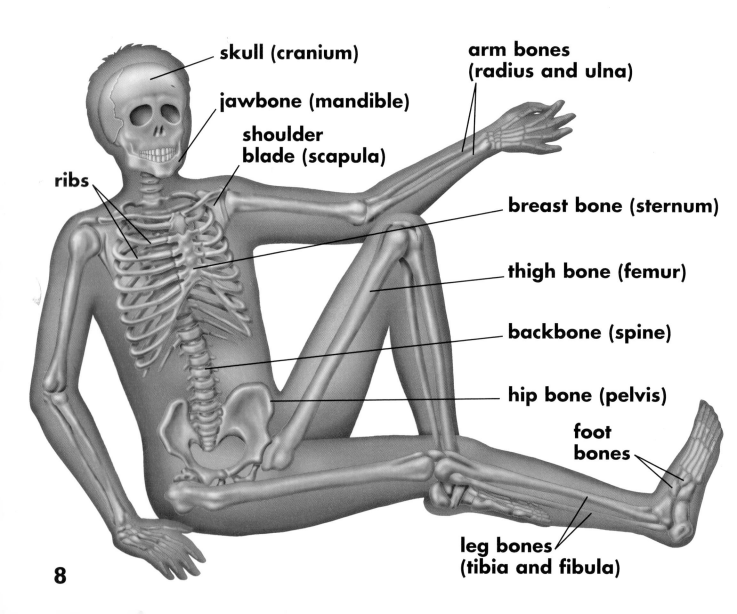

- skull (cranium)
- jawbone (mandible)
- shoulder blade (scapula)
- arm bones (radius and ulna)
- ribs
- breast bone (sternum)
- thigh bone (femur)
- backbone (spine)
- hip bone (pelvis)
- foot bones
- leg bones (tibia and fibula)

Your skeleton has a very important job. It holds your body up and gives you shape. Without your skeleton, your body would collapse in a heap. Your skeleton is very strong. It protects the soft parts of your body from injury. For example, your **skull** protects your delicate brain. Your ribs protect your heart and lungs. Your skeleton also helps you move. Your bones and your muscles work together so you can run, jump, and play basketball.

As your bones grow, you get taller. How tall are you now? Can you guess how tall you will be when you finish growing?

What's Inside a Bone?

Your bones are made of water and hard, stony **calcium**. Bones can bend a little because they are not solid all the way through. The outside of a bone is very hard and stiff, but the inside of a bone looks like a sponge made of calcium. This inner **spongy bone** makes your bones lighter in weight and gives them strength. Some bones have a jellylike material inside called **bone marrow**. It makes new blood cells for your blood.

Amazing!

The smallest bones in your body are hidden deep inside your ears. They are only the size of grains of rice. These bones help you hear.

Bone marrow makes new blood cells.

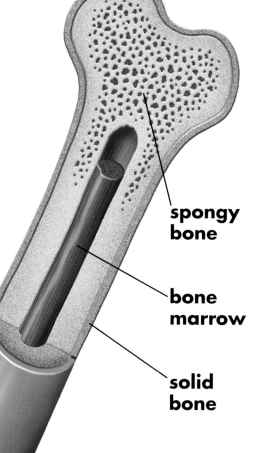

spongy bone

bone marrow

solid bone

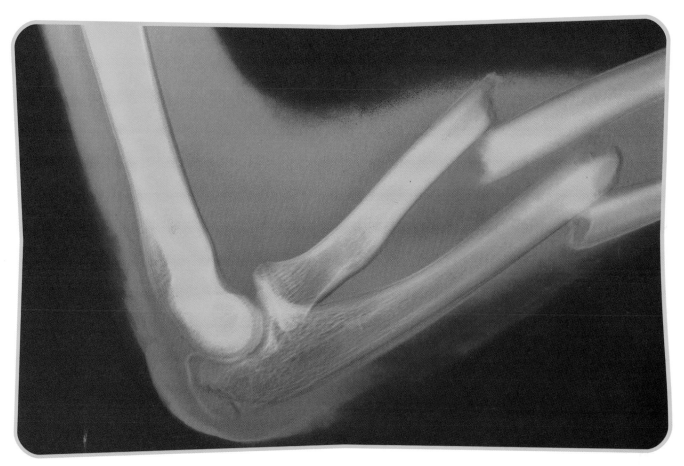

This X ray shows an elbow **joint** and some broken bones in the lower arm.

Sometimes bones break, but they can repair themselves. Special photographs called **X rays** let doctors look at the bones inside your body. When doctors see the shape of a broken bone, they know how to help that bone repair itself. A broken bone might need a plaster cast to help it heal properly.

Gently press on your knee, your elbow, or your chin, and you will feel one of your brilliant bones.

Moving Bones

Your bones are strong and stiff, so why is your body so flexible? Many of your bones meet at places called joints, such as your elbows, shoulders, and knees. You have about 100 joints in your body. Joints let your bones move so that you can twist, turn, and bend. Just think — without elbow joints, you would have to hold your arms straight out, all the time!

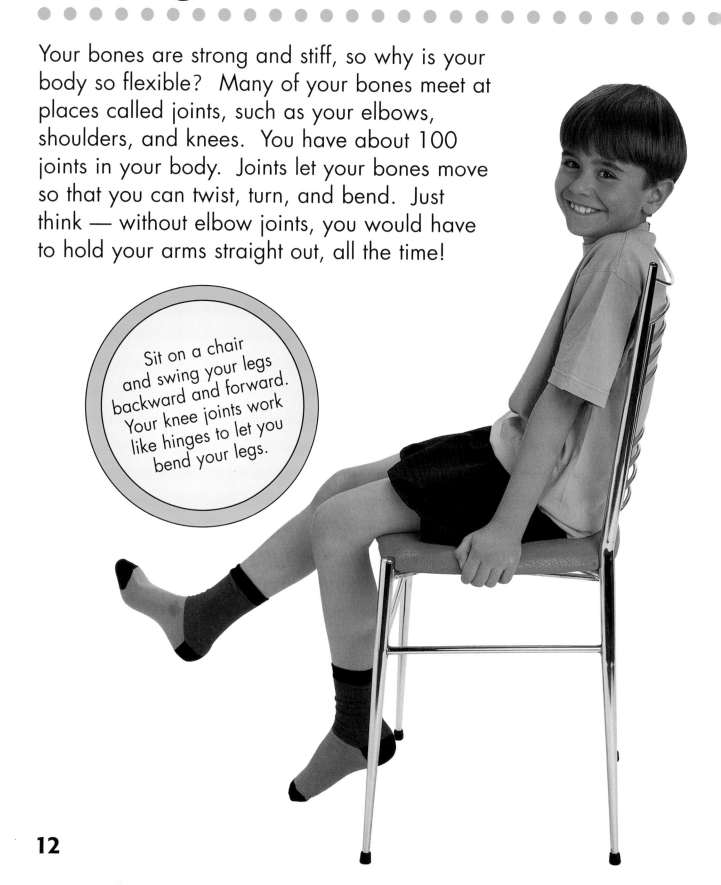

Sit on a chair and swing your legs backward and forward. Your knee joints work like hinges to let you bend your legs.

Bones in a joint do not usually touch each other. The ends of the bones are covered with soft, tough pads that stop bones from rubbing together. A special liquid also keeps the joint slippery. Bones in a joint are attached to each other by strong, stretchy straps called **ligaments**.

Your elbow and knee joints work like door hinges that move back and forth. But your hip is a ball-and-socket joint. It lets you swing your legs around in a circle.

Your hip joint fits together like a ball and socket.

Heads and Tails

Your skull is a hollow, bony case at the top of your body. One of your skull's main jobs is to protect your delicate brain. The bones in your skull are joined together like jigsaw puzzle pieces. When you were born, your skull was soft and squishy to help you squeeze out of your mother's body. As you got older, your skull turned into hard, strong bone.

The only part of your skull that moves is your **jawbone**. Your jawbone lets you bite, chew, talk, and yawn.

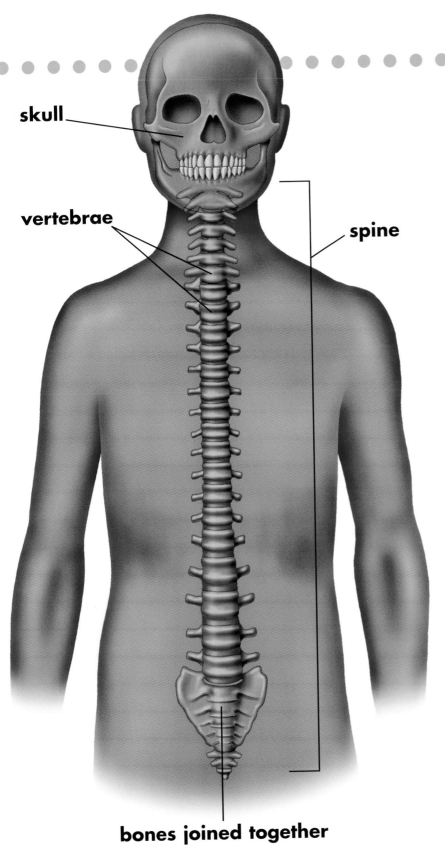

skull

vertebrae

spine

bones joined together

A long chain of bones forms your **backbone**, or **spine**. Your spine has 26 bones called **vertebrae**. They are linked together to help you twist, bend, walk, and run. The many vertebrae of your spine also protect a delicate bundle of nerves, called your **spinal cord**, from injury. Your skull sits on the top two bones of your spine. The lowest bones in your spine join to form a short tail.

Amazing!

A giraffe's neck has only seven bones. That's the same number of bones you have in your neck!

Your Muscles

You have hundreds of muscles under your skin. Some of them are small and delicate. Other muscles are large and powerful. Your muscles are connected to your bones by strong bands called **tendons**. The thickest and strongest tendon in your body is between your heel and lower leg. It is called the **Achilles tendon**. This tendon helps you stand on your toes.

buttocks
muscles

muscles in
back of legs

Amazing!

Your biggest muscles are in your **buttocks** and the upper part of your legs. These strong muscles help you walk and run.

Achilles
tendons

Not all muscles move bones. Muscles deep inside your body make your heart beat and your lungs breathe. Other muscles help you **digest** your food. Tiny muscles in your face move your skin to make you smile or frown.

Muscles get bigger and stronger when you use them a lot. Many **athletes** exercise daily to strengthen their muscles.

You can see and feel some of the muscles in your body. Bend your elbow and feel your upper arm. This muscle is called your **biceps**.

Muscles at Work

A muscle must shorten, or **contract**, to make a bone move. A muscle that moves a bone can only work one way, so muscles that move bones must work in pairs. One muscle shortens to move a bone in one direction. Then another muscle on the opposite side of that bone contracts to pull the bone back again.

Amazing!

Your smallest muscles are deep inside your ears. They move the tiny ear bones that help you hear different noises.

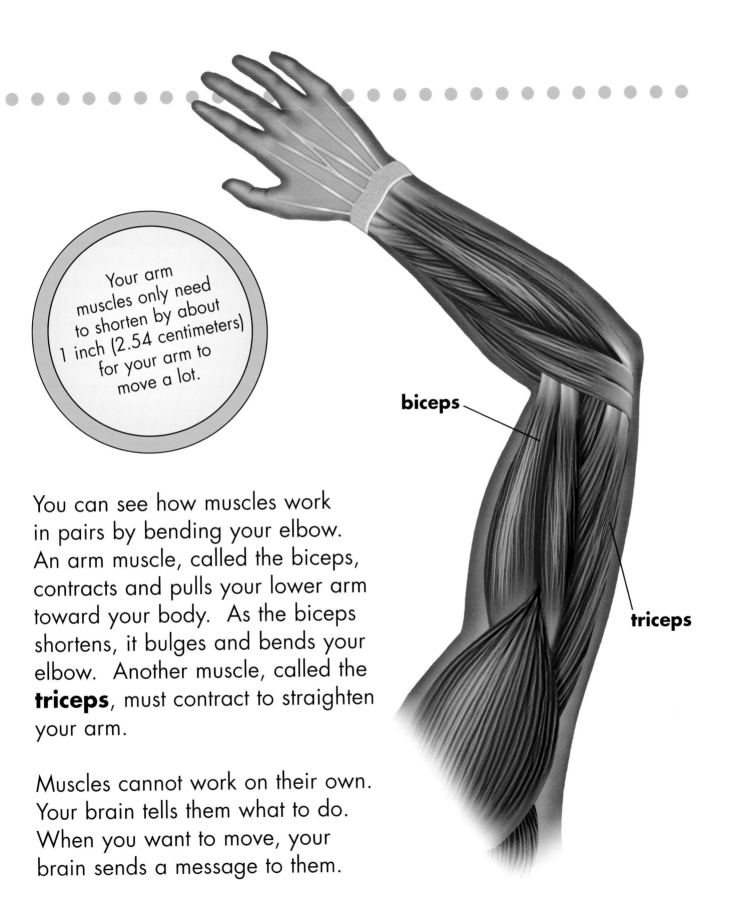

Your arm muscles only need to shorten by about 1 inch (2.54 centimeters) for your arm to move a lot.

biceps

triceps

You can see how muscles work in pairs by bending your elbow. An arm muscle, called the biceps, contracts and pulls your lower arm toward your body. As the biceps shortens, it bulges and bends your elbow. Another muscle, called the **triceps**, must contract to straighten your arm.

Muscles cannot work on their own. Your brain tells them what to do. When you want to move, your brain sends a message to them.

Inside a Muscle

Your muscles are made of very thin **fibers**, like tiny, stretchy, elastic bands. Each of these fibers is made of even finer threads. When all of your muscle fibers act together and contract, your muscle changes shape. Each muscle stays in its right place inside your body because of a special stretchy skin covering it.

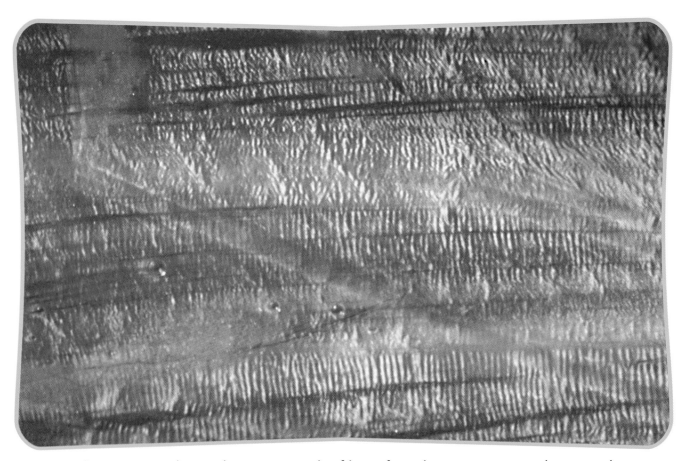

A **microscope** shows the tiny, stretchy fibers found in your arm or leg muscles.

Muscles need lots of energy to make them work. They get energy from the food you eat and from the oxygen you breathe. Your blood carries the food and oxygen all over your body to your hard-working muscles.

Sometimes your muscles are working hard but do not get enough energy. When a muscle does not get the energy it needs, it might give you a **cramp**. A cramp makes the muscle suddenly feel painful, tight, and stuck in place. You must gently stretch the muscle to stop it from hurting.

You can help prevent muscle cramps by gently stretching your muscles before, during, and after exercising.

Hands and Feet

Your hands and feet are amazing. Think how many things you can do with them. You can write a letter, play the piano, and even twiddle your thumbs. You can run, jump, kick a football, and stand on your tiptoes.

Your arms have big, strong muscles and bones. They help you climb a tree or carry heavy items, such as a stack of books. Your hands have lots of small bones and muscles. They let your fingers make delicate movements, such as typing on a keyboard.

Your thumbs are more useful than you might think. Try picking up a coin without using your thumb. It's trickier than it seems.

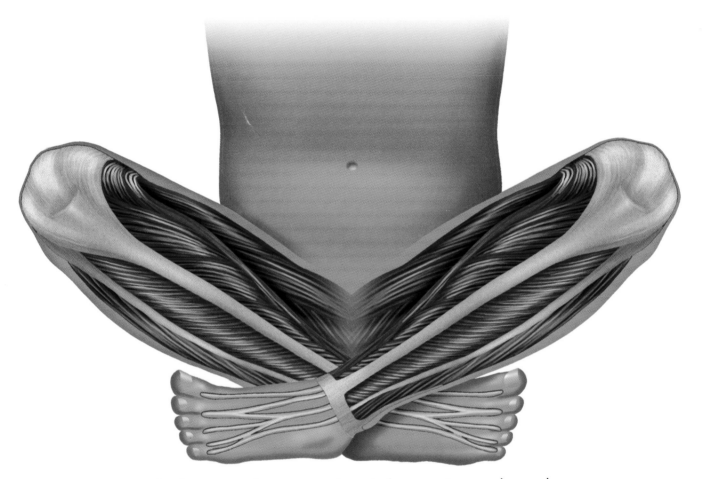

The long muscles in your legs help you sit cross-legged.

Amazing!

Your longest muscle runs down your leg from your hip to your knee.

Your legs and feet are built in a similar way to your arms and hands. Your legs are very long and strong. They support the weight of your body. Many muscles from your buttocks, upper and lower legs, feet, and even your toes work together when you stand, walk, and run.

Funny Faces

Look in a mirror and stick out your tongue. Smile. Frown. Wrinkle your nose. Every time you make a face, you use lots of different muscles. Your face muscles do not move bones. Instead, they pull on your skin to make your face move. Every muscle in your face has a special job, such as helping you smile.

Six muscles around your eyeballs let you **swivel** your eyes around.

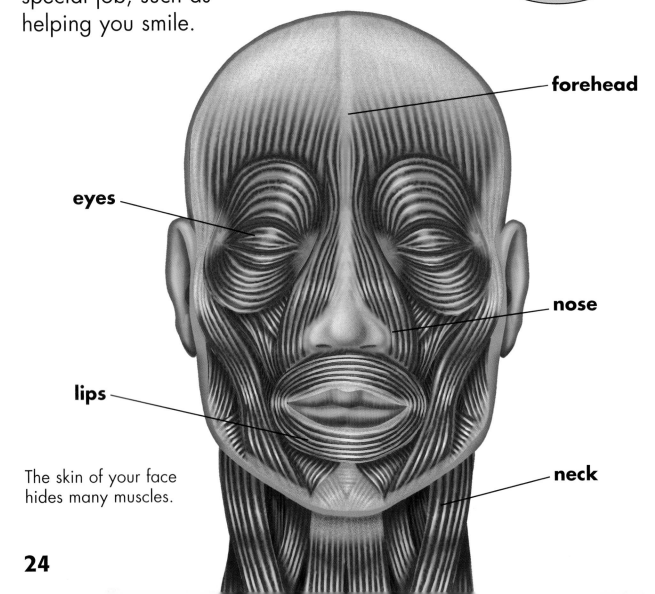

forehead

eyes

nose

lips

neck

The skin of your face hides many muscles.

You make lots of funny faces every day. They help you show other people how you are feeling. Are you feeling grumpy, happy, or sad? All these faces are made by your muscles.

The busiest muscles in your face are in your eyelids. They work very fast to make you blink thousands of times a day. Blinking covers your eyes with tears. Your tears keep your eyes clean and help protect them from harm and injury.

Activity

Your skeleton has more than 200 bones. How many of the bones in your skeleton can you name? Photocopy page 27. Match the numbers below to the bones listed on page 27.

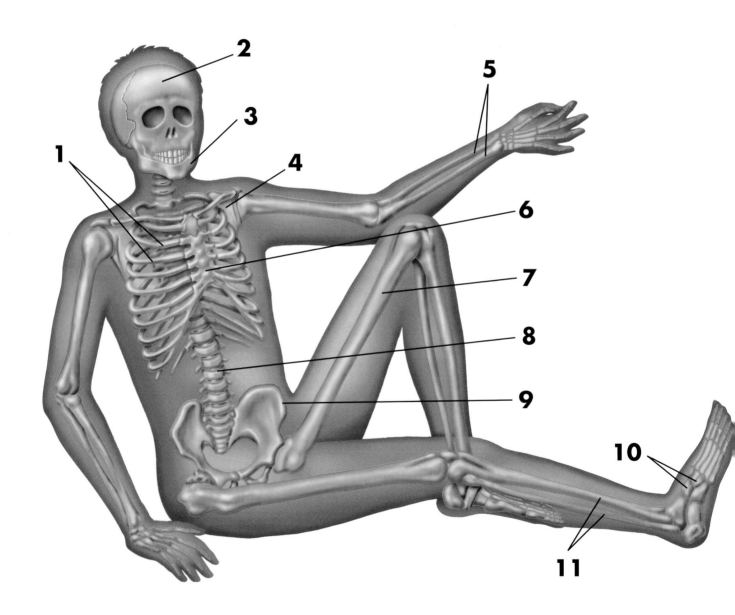

Do not write on this page.
Ask an adult to help you photocopy this page, then write your answers on the photocopy. (See page 8 to check your answers.)

_____ **breast bone**

_____ **hip bone**

_____ **skull**

_____ **ribs**

_____ **foot bones**

_____ **jawbone**

_____ **arm bones**

_____ **thigh bone**

_____ **leg bones**

_____ **shoulder blade**

_____ **backbone (spine)**

Glossary

* *

Achilles tendon: the strong tendon that attaches your lower leg muscle to your heel.

athletes: people who train and exercise so that they get better at a sport or a game.

backbone: your spine, a column of 26 connected bones that runs down your back.

biceps: the muscle on the front of your upper arm that contracts when you bend your elbow.

bone marrow: a jellylike material found inside some of your bones. It makes new blood cells.

bones: very hard parts inside your body that hold you up and protect soft body parts.

buttocks: the fleshy part of your body you sit on.

calcium: a hard, stony mineral that helps form your bones.

contract: to shorten.

cramp: a sharp pain you feel when a muscle suddenly squeezes very tight.

digest: to break down food into tiny pieces that your blood can carry through your entire body.

fibers: very tiny, fine threads that can look like wires.

jawbone: the lower bone of your skull. It is the only part of your skull that moves.

joint: the place where two bones meet, such as in your knees and shoulders.

ligaments: stretchy straps that connect one bone to another bone in a joint.

microscope: an instrument used to look at objects that are too tiny to see with just your eyes alone.

muscles: soft tissues that contract to move body parts.

nerves: the special cells that look like thin threads or wires and carry messages between your body and your brain.

skeleton: the many bones that form the shape of your body.

skull: the hard case of bone that forms your head and moveable jawbone.

spinal cord: the thick bundle of nerves that runs down your back inside the bones of your spine, or backbone.

spine: your backbone, a chain of 26 bones that runs down your back.

spongy bone: the inside layer of a bone that looks like a sponge but is made of a hard mineral called calcium.

swivel: to turn in many directions while staying in one spot.

tendons strong bands that attach muscles to bones.

thigh: the area of your legs between your hips and knees.

triceps: the muscle on the back of your upper arm that contracts to straighten your elbow.

vertebrae: the 26 individual bones that link together to form your spine, or backbone.

X rays: special photographs used to look at the bones inside your body.

More Books to Read

Bones. Body Books (series).
Anna Sandeman
(Copper Beech Books)

Bones: Our Skeletal System.
Seymour Simon
(Morrow Junior)

Dem Bones. Bob Barner
(Chronicle Books)

Muscles: Our Muscular System.
Seymour Simon
(Morrow Junior)

The Muscular System. Human
Body Systems (series).
Helen Frost (Pebble Books)

The Skeleton Inside You. Let's-
Read-and-Find-Out (series).
Philip Balestrino (HarperTrophy)

Videos

All About Bones & Muscles.
(Schlessinger Media)

The Incredible Human Machine.
(National Geographic)

Web Sites

*BrainPOP: Muscular System.
How Do Our Bodies Move?*
www.brainpop.com/health/
muscular/muscular/

Dancing Bones.
www.scottforesman.com/
resources/health/hbones.html

Index